Joke Busters

MONSTER MANIA

JOHN BYRNE

For Laura Michelle Kelly –
powerful enough to defeat any monster

Scholastic Children's Books,
Commonwealth House, 1–19 New Oxford Street,
London WC1A 1NU, UK
A division of Scholastic Ltd
London ~ New York ~ Toronto ~ Sydney ~ Auckland
Mexico City ~ New Delhi ~ Hong Kong

Published in the UK by Scholastic Ltd, 2003

Text and illustrations copyright © John Byrne, 2003

ISBN 0 439 97739 8

All rights reserved
Printed by Nørhaven Paperback A/S, Denmark

2 4 6 8 10 9 7 5 3 1

The right of John Byrne to be identified as the author and illustrator
of this work has been asserted by him in accordance with
the Copyright, Designs and Patents Act, 1988.

WELCOME TO JOKE BUSTERS HEADQUARTERS! IT'S OUR MISSION TO COLLECT THE BEST MONSTER JOKES IN THE WORLD AND PUT THEM IN THIS BOOK...

...AND WE NEED YOUR HELP TO DO IT!

AGENT GIGGLE

AGENT GROAN

But before we begin, we need to test your comedy credentials. Turn the page for the...

OFFICIAL Joke Busters SECURITY CHECK!

OFFICIAL
Joke Busters
SECURITY CHECK!

1 When face to face with a horrible monster, do you:

a) Scream
b) Run
c) Say "Gosh, I didn't know our headmaster had a twin!"

2 Who is your favourite monster?

a) Dracula
b) Frankenstein
c) Whichever monster is asking me the question

3 What is your favourite monster joke?

a) The joke about the invisible monster (although a lot of people don't see the point)
b) The joke about the monster massage (although it rubs people up the wrong way)
c) I'd be very careful about telling monster jokes – the monster might not have a sense of humour!

• CONGRATULATIONS! •

You got all the answers right! (Mainly because there aren't any wrong answers!) We're proud to have you join our mission – and you'll be a monster joke expert by the time we're finished!

LET'S GET JOKE BUSTING!

WHY WOULDN'T THE MUMMY BUY A HALF-FINISHED PYRAMID?

BECAUSE IT WOULD BE POINTLESS.

WHERE DO YOU PUT A MUMMY WITH A SORE THROAT?

IN A SAR-COUGH-AGUS!

Little Miss Mummy
Was feeding her tummy,
Said a spider, "Her snack I
 will nick..."
But her curds were all cold,
And 3,000 years old.
Now the spider's gone
 off to be sick.

YEUCH! I FEEL A BIT WOBBLY ROUND THE LEGS, LEGS LEGS, LEGS...

8

THAT'S WHAT YOU GET FOR TRYING TO READ RUNNY LETTERING, AGENT GIGGLE! THIS ISN'T "THE MUMMY'S CURSE", IT'S "THE MUMMY'S NURSE"! SHE'S BEEN TRYING TO PUT HIM TO SLEEP FOR CENTURIES AND YOU WOKE HIM UP AGAIN!

NUMBER 1 SOCKULA!

Where does it lurk?
Bottom of gym bag, bedroom floor, under Christmas tree.

Does it make you sweat?
Actually it's sweaty enough all by itself. (Yeuch!)

What's it scared of?
The washing machine (not that it's in there very often).

π
?
WHIFF!
PONG!
REEK!

> AARGH! HIS MONSTER POWERS ARE NOT TO BE SNIFFED AT!

14

MONSTERS in FOCUS

Name: Invisible Man

Habitat: Right behind you, for all you know.

Favourite Food: Why ask? Look in my tummy and there it is!

Favourite Film: All of them. (I can slip in and take a seat without paying.)

Least Favourite Film: The ones where people sit on me 'cos they don't know I'm on the seat!

Favourite Joke: What did one Invisible Man say to the other? I haven't seen you round here lately...

MONSTER TIMES

INSIDE: FULL **TV** GUIDE!
("TV" IS SHORT FOR TRANSYLVAINIA)

GIVE BLOOD TODAY!

DRACULA LEADS BLOOD DONOR DRIVE!

Count Dracula was named as the person leading a huge drive for blood donors. The Blood Donors Association are not pleased – they have insisted he turn off his hypnotic stare and stop leading the blood donors up the drive to his castle so they can return to giving blood at the local hospital like they're supposed to.

WARNING!

IF YOU ARE IN ANY WAY

DO NOT TURN THE PAGE

AS YOU WILL SEE AN EXCLUSIVE PICTURE OF A

IN FULL 'ORRIBLE DETAIL

20

21

MONSTER

MUNCHIES!

23

Joke Busters
Guide to
REAL MONSTERS

2 WERE-WORDS!

Where does it lurk?
In your schoolbag ... or at least it
should have been.

Yes... I'm the ESSAY you were supposed to write for homework but you forgot!

Does it scare you?
Not as much as the
5,000 lines you'll have
to write for not doing
your homework.

What's it scared of?
The dog eating it ...
at least that's what
you're thinking of
telling teacher.

*THAT'S ONE ADVANTAGE OF BEING
A WEREWOLF AT SCHOOL... WHEN
THE FULL MOON COMES OUT YOU
CAN EAT YOUR OWN HOMEWORK.*

MONSTERS in FOCUS

Name: Mr Hyde

Habitat: Dr Jekyll's laboratory.

Favourite Food: Dr Jekyll's transformation potion.

Favourite Film: The one on top of Dr Jekyll's transformation potion... We shouldn't have left it standing out so long.

Least Favourite Film: Any one where I can't get two tickets for the price of one.

Favourite Joke: What do you get when you cross Dr Jekyll with a mouse? Hyde and Squeak!

31

THE "🦇" VAMPIRE

JOKE FILE

MEMO TO AGENT GIGGLE: SORRY THE PHOTO IS SO DARK. BUT THE VAMPIRE GOT VERY STROPPY WHEN I SUGGESTED GOING OUT INTO THE SUNLIGHT TO GET A BETTER SHOT. AGENT GROAN

WHAT DID ONE VAMPIRE BAT SAY TO THE OTHER VAMPIRE BAT?

YOU CAN - COUNT ON ME!

WHY DID THE VAMPIRE DRINK HONEY AND LEMON?

TO HELP HIS COFFIN'

WHICH VAMPIRE IS REALLY GOOD AT SNOOKER?

DRA-CUE-LA!

Two little vampires, sitting on a wall,
Forgot to check when the sun would call.
"It's your fault," said Peter in disgust...
But by then you couldn't see him or Paul for dust.

WHAT'S GOT INDIGESTION AND SCARES DRACULA?

BURPY THE VAMPIRE SLAYER.

WHAT DO YOU CALL A CHEAP VAMPIRE?

DIS-COUNT DRACULA!

WANTED:

COUNT DRACULA
SEEKS EXPERIENCED
ASSISTANT VAMPIRES

If you've got your bat-flapping licence and a
thirst for work you can get your teeth into,
Count Dracula would like to hear from you.
Thanks to the Joke Busters team locking up
many of my best vampires I am badly in
need of fresh blood.

Joke Buster's
GALLERY OF FOES

EXCLUSIVE FREE GIFT FOR ALL READERS:

LIMITED EDITION

LIFE-SIZE POSTER

OF

LOOK OUT FOR THE REST OF THIS LIMITED EDITION SOON.

ACTUALLY, SINCE THIS LIMITED EDITION IS LIMITED TO THIS BIT ONLY, MAYBE YOU SHOULDN'T BOTHER ...

NUMBER 3 SINISTER SCHOOL DINNER!

Where does it lurk?
The school canteen ... especially if you don't get in the queue fast enough.

Does it give you a sinking feeling in your stomach?
Oh yes ... and that's even before you've eaten it.

What's it scared of?
A decent recipe book.

AT LAST!

AFTER MONTHS OF
BACKBREAKING DETECTIVE
WORK, AGENT GIGGLE
AND AGENT GROAN
CAN BRING YOU THE FIRST-
EVER PICTURE OF THE ...

LOCH
NESS
MONSTER!

THE Jekyll and HYDE JOKE FILE

THIS WAS ONE OF THE HARDEST FILES TO DO. FIRST DR JEKYLL SAID HE'D HELP, THEN SOMEONE ELSE TURNED UP. I THINK HE'S QUITE TWO-FACED! AGENT GROAN

WHAT DOES MR HYDE PLAY IN THE PARK?

HYDE AND GO SHRIEK!

WHAT'S HAIRY, LIVES IN THE DESERT AND TURNS INTO A MONSTER?

DR JACKAL!

Old King Cole was a merry old soul,
And a merry old soul was he,
Until he drank Dr Jekyll's potion...

MONSTERS in FÔCUS

Name: Cerberus the Three-Headed Dog

Habitat: Gates of the Underworld AKA Hades. (He's a Hot Dog!)

Favourite Food: Dog food. (Well, two out of three heads prefer it.)

Favourite Film: I never get to see them ... there's always someone's head in front.

Favourite Joke: How does Cerberus treat postmen? Ruff!

50

55

Joke Busters
Guide to
REAL MONSTERS

NUMBER **4** DOCUMENTARY OF DOOM!

WAVES OF BOREDOM

STAND BY FOR AN HOUR LONG LOOK AT BASKET-WEAVING IN MONGOLIA!

Where does it lurk?
On the other channel at exactly the same time as your favourite cartoon.

Does it scare you?
Yes ... especially the thought that some day you might be like your parents and prefer stuff.

What's it scared of?
Who knows ... after five minutes you're too fast asleep to notice.

222

MONSTERS in FOCUS

Name: Kraken

Habitat: The depths of the ocean.

Favourite Food: Seafood, of course. (And sailors who've gone off course!)

Favourite Film: Jaws 5

Hang on! There wasn't a Jaws 5: I know – that's how many sharks I eat for breakfast.

Favourite Joke: What did the Kraken say to the shark? Mmm ... delicious.

MONSTER MIRROR

LOCH NESS MONSTER SPOTTED!

The Loch Ness Monster was spotted today. "It's terrible," she said. "I've had these spots since yesterday evening. All over my body, before my eyes, spots everywhere I look. Maybe I'm allergic to porridge!" When asked if she had seen a vet she replied, "No. Just spots."

YOU CAN'T HAVE A JOKE BOOK WITHOUT KNOCK KNOCK JOKES...

...SO TURN THE PAGE FOR OUR JUMBO COLLECTION OF...

MONSTER KNOCK KNOCKS!

66

Joke Buster's
Guide to
REAL MONSTERS

NUMBER
5 JOBZILLA!

Where does it lurk?
The garden shed, the local shops, the attic. This horror is all those boring chores you have to do when you'd much rather be doing something else.

Does it scare you?
It certainly leaves you feeling empty ... because if you don't do your chores, there's no pocket money!

What's it scared of?
You – 'cos the only way to get out of these terrible tasks is to do them badly so you won't be asked again. (Or get made to do them until you get them right... Don't say we didn't warn you!)

MONSTERS in FÔCUS

Name: Yeti

Habitat: Himalayas.

Favourite Food: Ice cream. (Also the van and guy selling it.)

Favourite Film: Snow White and the Six Dwarfs.

Shouldn't that be "Seven Dwarfs"? Sorry – I got a bit peckish.

Favourite Joke: Why did the Yeti cross the road? He was frozen to the chicken.

THE ABOMINABLE JOKE FILE

ABOMINABLE SNOWMAN
WARNING!

WE HAVE REASON TO BELIEVE A HERD OF ABOMINABLE SNOW PEOPLE HAVE HIDDEN THEMSELVES IN THE WHITE BITS OF THESE PAGES. IN CASE THEY TRY TO ESCAPE, USE THESE HANDY TIPS TO PROTECT YOUR BEDROOM AND PROPERTY.

TIP 1

You'll know an Abominable Snowman's been in your room because there will be **FUR** everywhere!

AND WHAT'S WRONG WITH THAT? I'VE GOT FUR EVERYWHERE AND YOU DON'T HEAR ME COMPLAINING!

TIP 2

You'll know an Abominable Snowman's been in your room because they leave footprints.

YES WE KNOW IT'S JUST ONE PRINT...THEY DON'T CALL HIM "BIGFOOT" FOR NOTHING!

TIP 3

You'll know an Abominable Snowman's been in your room because there will be a note from the Abominable Snowman:

SORRY I COULDN'T STAY...BUT WHEN I SAW THAT THE ROOM WAS MESSY ENOUGH TO LEAVE FOOTPRINTS IN... WELL I DON'T KNOW WHY THEY CALL **ME** "ABOMINABLE"!

HORRIBLE

AGENTS GIGGLE AND GROAN AREN'T THE ONLY ONES WHO HAVE A BIG BOOK COLLECTION! US MONSTERS LIKE FILLING UP WITH FEARSOME FACTS TOO!
FOILING THE INVISIBLE MAN BY I. SEEHIM
WHO WILL MONSTERS EAT? BY N.E. BODY
I'M NOT SCARED OF MONSTERS BY HUGH CARES
SMALL MONSTERS BY PIP SQUEAK

HOMEWORK!

NUMBER
6 **LITTLE BROTHER!**

(* CAN ALSO BE A LITTLE SISTER)

Where does it lurk?
It follows you wherever you go!

Does it scare you?
Yes ... especially when Mum tells you that you used to be like that once, too.

What's it scared of?
Nothing ... after all it's got a big brother or sister like you to look after it!

MONSTERS in FÔCUS

Name: Troll

Habitat: Monster Mountain.

Favourite Food: Mountaineers.

Favourite Film: Lord of the Honks

Shouldn't that be "Lord of the Rings"? No — I don't need bells now that my horns are working.

Favourite Joke: What did one mountain say to the other mountain? No peak-ing.

MONSTER A TO Z

MONSTER A TO Z

C IS FOR CREATURE FROM THE SWAMP!

WHY ARE SWAMP CREATURES SO BUSY?

'COS THEY'RE ALWAYS GETTING BOGGED DOWN IN THEIR WORK!

D IS FOR DRACULA!

WHERE'S DRACULA'S FAVOURITE DISCO?

DANCE-SYLVANIA!

MONSTER A to Z

MONSTER A TO Z

MONSTER A TO Z

K IS FOR KRAKEN!

WHY DO KRAKENS MAKE GOOD SEA MONSTERS?

BECAUSE AS SOON AS I "SEA" ONE, I'M OFF!

L IS FOR LOCH NESS!

WHAT'S SCOTTISH AND TELLS THE TIME?

THE CLOCK NESS MONSTER

M IS FOR MUMMY!

WHAT DO YOU CALL A VAMPIRE MUMMY?

TOOTHY-KHAMUN!

MONSTER A TO Z

N IS FOR NIGHTMARES!

HOW DO YOU GET A MONSTER TO WAKE UP SCREAMING?

WISH HIM "SWEET DREAMS."

O IS FOR OGRE!

HOW DO YOU KNOW AN OGRE IS A BIG BABY?

'COS HE SUCKS HIS FEE-FI-FO FUMB!

MONSTER A to Z

MONSTER A TO Z

S IS FOR SCREAM!

HOW DO MONSTERS DIVIDE A BAG OF SWEETS?

EEK-QUALY!

SWEETS

T IS FOR TROLL!

WHAT'S SCARY, COVERED IN PASTRY AND LIVES IN THE MOUNTAINS?

A SAUSAGE TROLL.

MONSTER A TO Z

U IS FOR UGLY!

WHAT DOES A MONSTER SAY WHEN YOU CALL HIM "UGLY"?

"FLATTERY WILL GET YOU NOWHERE!"

V IS FOR VAMPIRE!

WHY DO VAMPIRES' DENTISTS WORK HARD?

SO THEY DON'T GET IT IN THE NECK FROM THEIR CUSTOMERS!

MONSTER A TO Z

W IS FOR WEREWOLF!

WHAT DO WEREWOLVES TAKE TO BED?

THEIR TEDDY WERES

X IS FOR X-CLUSIVE INTERVIEW WITH A VAMPIRE!

OH NO, IT ISN'T! I'M MUCH TOO SHY! I'M HEADING FOR THE "X-IT"!

MONSTER A TO Z

Y IS FOR YETI!

HEY! HOW COME WE YETIS DIDN'T MAKE IT TILL THE END OF THE DICTIONARY?

WE TRIED TO GET IN EARLIER, BUT WE GOT A FROSTY RECEPTION!

Z IS FOR ZZZZ ZZZZ

SORRY... GOT TIRED OF WAITING FOR YOU LOT TO GET HERE. I'VE GONE FOR MY BEAUTY SLEEP. *

* AND MONSTERS NEED ALL THE BEAUTY SLEEP THEY CAN GET!

CONGRATULATIONS!

You have successfully made it through Monster Mania and have earned your official Joke Busters ID card: